# From the Sealed Box

## Simply French

### A French Christmas

## VOL. IV

### by Dion Jones-Lewin

# AP

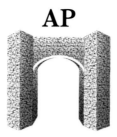

## AN ARCHBURY PRESS BOOK

Created and Produced by
**Archbury Press**
Post Office Box 20668
Boulder, CO 80308

*Editorial Director* Dion Jones-Lewin
*Art Director/Photographer* Jenny Orin
*Hairstylist* Mary Kay Gilson from Tresca
Boulder Garden Florist
Liquor Mart
Cheese Importers

Published in the United States by Archbury Press

ISBN# 978-0-615-90212-8

A catalog record is available from the Library of Congress

Printed and bound by Eight Days a Week in Boulder, Colorado

*"French cuisine is considered too difficult and time-consuming for the average person to prepare. Nothing could be further from the truth. My grand-mère, Germaine Dethiere-Jones, taught me otherwise."*

1926

1944

# Germaine Dethière-Jones
1898-1989

*From top to bottom:*

*1. Noël in Paris with my daughter, Francine,*

   *and my sisters, Christine and Françoise. 1971*

*2. Francine dressed as a flight attendant with Christine. Paris, 1971*

# Table of Contents

# Introduction

*Noël,* or Christmas, was always a very special time for my *grand-mère* and me. We both loved what the holiday represents: family, good food, friends, and great feelings of comfort and security. While writing Volume IV, *A French Christmas,* those feelings were brought back to me. I know that *Grand-mère* is next to me in my kitchen as I prepare her recipes. The smells bring me back to my youth in Paris. I remember *Grand-mère* planning her Christmas menu two months in advance. Everything from the food to the table decorations had to be perfect. I hope that, with these very special recipes, you can create great memories with your family that will last for generations.

As my readers know, I learned the art of French cooking from my grandmother, who learned from her mother and grandmother. It is because of my *grand-mère* that I love to cook, and this cookbook series was inspired by an unexpected gift I found years after her death; amongst her belongings was a sealed box filled with my grandmother's collection of recipes and old photographs. To me, it is a treasure trove, offering not only the delicious food that reminds me of family meals, but also a glimpse into my family history. This cookbook was written for those readers who have little time for lengthy meal preparation.

This cookbook series began during the savage fighting of World War I, when my *grand-mère,* Germaine Dethière, a young girl from Arras, met a British sergeant named Wyalt Jones. Though neither spoke the other's language, they soon fell in love and married immediately after the Armistice. Because of the post-war recession in England and because Germaine spoke no English, the couple elected to remain in France. Soon, my father Walter and his brother Marcel were born.

Germaine learned to cook from her mother and grandmother, both of whom were trained in classic French cooking, so she decided to use her skills professionally. For the next ten years she held jobs in various *auberges* in northern France, where she refined her technique. During the Great Depression of the 1930's, she accepted a position as the executive chef at the Standard Athletic Club in Meudon-la Forêt, an exclusive British country club outside Paris, where she worked until the German occupation of France during World War II. It was there she developed a collection of easy-to-prepare classic French meals, which she later taught me as I stood alongside her in the kitchen.

In 1941, because Germaine was the wife of a British citizen, the Gestapo arrested and imprisoned her in *Frontstalag* 141, an interment camp near the Swiss border. My grandfather, who had became the Standard Athletic Club's grounds manager, was also arrested by the Gestapo and sent to *Frontstalag* 142, at St-Denis near Paris. My *grand-mère* was released after 6 months of imprisonment, but my *grand-père* was held prisoner until the Allied Liberation of Paris in 1944. Their children, however, managed to escape France. My father joined the Free French Army in Niger, West Africa, and my uncle served in the Royal Air Force in England.

Amid the chaos of the end of the war, my grandparents found each other once more. The Standard Athletic Club had been destroyed during the fighting, so they decided to move to England. Germaine's culinary expertise quickly got her a job cooking in a exclusive boarding school for girls.

I was born in Paris in 1947, but it was there in England during my summer vacations where I first learned the art of French cooking. I can still see myself standing on a stool by the stove handing *Grand-mère* the salt and pepper and trying to reach for the wooden spoon to taste the sauce. In a short time I was preparing simple French meals by myself, as well as classic British fish and chips, which to this day I still love to make. Not only did *Grand-mère* inspire my cooking, but she also taught me to drive her British sports car, an MG TC Roadster with wire wheels and right-hand drive. I think I ground the gears a few times, but it was fun.

Later on, after *Grand-père* passed away, *Grand-mère* moved back to Paris, and I would visit her on weekends while I completed my formal training in French cooking. This inspired me to open a French culinary school, Ecole de Cuisine, in Boulder, Colorado after moving here in the 1980's. The school trained several hundred students in *"La Methode,"* the art of French cuisine.

This cookbook series is dedicated to Germaine Jones' technique of creating simple, mouthwatering French meals quickly. I translated all the recipes from the original French and converted the measurements from metric to English units. All recipes call for commonly available ingredients. There are 30 delicious, easy-to-prepare recipes for all occasions. Working with a professional photographer, I have personally prepared each dish from the recipe as it appears in this cookbook. The photographs are of the actual results, no artificial substitutes were used.

As my readers know, I purposely designed the size of all my cookbooks to fit into a handbag or a tote, thus making the cookbook convenient to carry when shopping for the foods necessary to prepare my recipes.

My website, www.CafeDion.com is designed to accompany my cookbook series. There you will find an informative cooking blog dedicated to French cooking made simple.

*Merci et à bientôt!* Thanks! I hope you enjoy this new cookbook.

*Dion Jones-Lewin*
BOULDER, COLORADO

*Grand-mère and friends,*
*Noël in Viry-Châtillon, Paris, 1986*

# Christmas Breakfast in the Library

# Mimosas
## Mimosas

SERVES: 6

TIME: 5 MINUTES + CHILLING

12 ounces fresh orange juice, chilled

1 bottle Champagne, cold

6 teaspoons orange liquor, like
Grand-Marnier or Triple Sec

6 mint leaves

1) Chill 6 flutes in freezer to frost the glasses.

2) Pour 2 ounces of orange juice into each glass
(⅓ of the glass).

3) Add Champagne.

4) Top each flute with a teaspoon of Grand-Marnier.

5) Decorate with a mint leaf.

# Café au Lait
## Coffee with Milk

SERVES: 6

TIME: 5 MINUTES

4 cups of black coffee, very hot

4 cups whole milk, very hot

Sugar

1) Fill each cup with ½ cup of coffee and ½ cup of milk.
Stir well. Add sugar.

2) Serve immediately.

# Brioches à la Confiture
## Buns with Jam

SERVES: 20
TIME: 1 HOUR + RISING
OVEN: 375 DEGREES

1½ sticks sweet butter, room temperature

3 large eggs, room temperature

⅔ cup warm milk (110-120 degrees)

⅔ cup water

1 tablespoon sugar

2½ teaspoons active yeast

3 tablespoons sugar

4½ cups bread flour, sifted

½ cup water

1½ teaspoons sea salt

1 egg mixed with 1 tablespoon milk

 (egg wash)

1) Whisk together butter and eggs in a bowl of a standard mixer on low speed until all combined (the mixture will look curdled, that OK), whisk in warmed milk.

2) Combine ⅔ cup water, 1 tablespoon sugar and yeast in a small bowl; set aside until foamy, 5-8 minutes.

3) Whisk together flour, ½ cup sugar, add salt in a bowl until well mixed. Add yeast mixture to butter mixture and knead on low speed with a dough hook attachment until dough is smooth and elastic, around 15 minutes. Transfer dough to a large, oiled bowl and cover with plastic wrap and let rise until doubled (1½ - 2 hours) or refrigerate overnight.

4) Punch down dough with your hand, to release the air, and divide into 20 portions.

5) Shape dough into balls and place on parchment paper-lined baking sheets.

6) Cover brioches with plastic wrap and let rise until double (1½ hours). Note: if you refrigerate the dough, this process with take longer.

7) Brush tops and sides of brioches with egg-wash mixture.

8) Bake until golden brown, 20-25 minutes in a preheated oven.

9) Cool on a wire rack

# Saucisses Maison
## Sausage Patties

2 pounds fresh ground pork or turkey

3 garlic cloves, minced

1 teaspoon ground sage

1 teaspoon fresh ground black pepper

⅛ teaspoon kosher salt

1 teaspoon dried oregano

1 teaspoon dried thyme

1 teaspoon cayenne pepper

1 tablespoon fresh lemon juice

2 tablespoons fresh parsley, chopped

3 tablespoons butter

1)  Mix first 10 ingredients using your fingers.

2)  Shape into 3-inch patties.

3)  Sauté in 3 tablespoons butter, until crisp and brown on both sides.

4)  Drain on paper towels.

5)  Serve immediately.

# Pommes de Terre Sautées à l'Ail
## Hash Browns

SERVES: 6
TIME: 35 MINUTES

10 medium Russet potatoes, peeled

8 ounces sweet butter

Salt and black pepper

4 garlic cloves, minced

5 tablespoons fresh parsley, chopped

1) Boil potatoes in plenty of boiling, salted water for 8 minutes.

2) Remove and rinse under cold water.

3) Cut potatoes in large chunks and dry them on paper towel.

4) Heat a quarter of the butter in a large skillet, sauté garlic on low heat for a minute, add potatoes, turning the potatoes often, add salt and pepper.

5) Cook for 15-20 minutes, by adding the remaining butter a tablespoon at a time. Potatoes should be a golden brown.

6) Garnish with parsley.

# Omelette à la Ciboulette
## Chive Omelet

SERVES: 6
TIME: 20 MINUTES

18 large eggs

6 tablespoons milk

4 tablespoons fresh chives, chopped

Salt and white pepper

8 tablespoons sweet butter

1) With a fork, whisk eggs and milk together. Add the chives and a pinch of salt and pepper, mix well.

2) Melt the butter in a large skillet and when the butter is foamy, pour in the egg mixture, tilting the pan and moving it around.

3) With a fork, keep lifting the cooked eggs around the edge so that the runny part in the center moves under the part that has set.

4) Repeat until the eggs have set underneath but are still creamy and a little runny on top.

5) Fold a third of the omelet towards the center and roll out onto a warmed plate, tilting the pan so that the omelet folds over again.

6) Serve immediately.

# Crêpe aux Fraises et Sauce au Chocolat
## Strawberry Pancake and Chocolate Sauce

SERVES: 6

TIME: 50 MINUTES

OVEN: 400 / 350 DEGREES

## CRÊPE:

6 large eggs

¾ cup whole milk

¼ teaspoon salt

4 tablespoon sugar

⅓ cup all-purpose flour, sifted

4 tablespoons sweet butter

## STRAWBERRY FILLING:

3 pints fresh strawberries, stems removed
  and halved

½ cup sugar

¼ cup orange liquor, like Grand-Marnier

## CHOCOLATE SAUCE:

¾ cup half and half

1 tablespoon sweet butter

½ pound semisweet chocolate chips
  (about 1⅓ cups)

¼ teaspoon vanilla extract

1 teaspoon espresso coffee, cold

1) **Make the Strawberry Filling:** stir strawberries and sugar together in a medium bowl, add Grand-Marnier Cover with plastic wrap and chill for 2 hours.

2) **Make the Chocolate Sauce:** Scald half and half and butter in a small saucepan over medium heat. Remove from heat.

3) Place the chocolate, vanilla and coffee in a medium heat-proof bowl. Add the hot half and half mixture and let sit for 2 minutes, then whisk until smooth. Serve warm.

4) **Make the *Crêpe*:** place oven rack in center of oven and preheat oven to 400 degrees. In a small bowl, whisk eggs and sugar, until combined. Whisk in milk, salt and flour. Set aside and let the batter rest for ½ hour.

5) Melt butter into a 10-inch deep-dish iron skillet. Place in the oven for 2 minutes or until butter is sizzling; quickly swirl to coat bottom and sides on pan. Immediately pour the pancake batter.

6) Bake for 15 minutes, if the bottom puffs up, prick it with a fork, reduce oven temperature to 350 degrees and continue baking for 8-10 minutes longer or until puffed and golden brown.

7) Remove from oven, lift out *crêpe* and place on a serving platter. Spoon strawberries in the center and top with chocolate sauce, and whipping cream, if desired.

8) Cut into wedges and serve immediately.

# Christmas Lunch

WINE SUGGESTION: BLANC DE BLANC
(SPARKLING WHITE WINE)

# Tarte au Jambon et Fromage
## Ham and Cheese Pie

SERVES: 8
TIME: 55 MINUTES
OVEN: 400 DEGREES

8 tablespoons Dijon mustard or honey

  mustard

1- 17.3-ounce package puff pastry, thawed

  (2 sheets)

½ pound cooked ham, thinly sliced

½ pound Swiss or Gruyère cheese,

  thinly sliced

½ cup parsley, chopped

1 egg and 1 tablespoon water (egg wash)

1) Preheat oven to 400 degrees. Line 2 baking sheets with parchment paper.

2) On a lightly floured surface, roll each sheet of puff pastry into a 15x12 inch rectangle.

3) Transfer each sheet to the prepared baking sheet.

4) Spread half of each pastry lengthwise with the mustard, leaving ½ inch border around outside edges.

5) Add individual layers of ham, and cheese over mustard.

6) In a small bowl, whisk together egg and water. Brush some of the egg wash on the uncovered edges of pastries.

7) Sprinkle parsley on top of cheese on each pastry.

8) Fold uncovered portion of each pastry rectangle up and over filling.

9) Use a fork to seal edges together. Brush tops with egg wash mixture.

10) Cut decorative slits in tops of each pastry for the steam to escape.

11) Bake in hot oven for 25 minutes or until pastries are golden on top and bottom.

12) Slide pies and parchment paper to a wire rack; cool slightly.

13) Cut into strips before serving.

# Paupiettes de Poulet aux Abricots Secs
## Chicken Breasts with Apricot Stuffing

SERVES: 8

TIME: 1 HOUR

½ cup dried apricots

1½ tablespoons currants

1½ tablespoons golden raisins

¾ cup chicken stock, low sodium, warmed

4 tablespoons sweet butter

½ cup shiitake mushrooms, finely chopped

½ cup button mushrooms, finely chopped

3 tablespoons shallots, chopped

1 cup fresh bread crumbs

3 tablespoons slivered almonds, toasted

1 tablespoon fresh sage, chopped

  or ½ teaspoon dried sage

1 tablespoon fresh thyme, chopped

½ cup fresh parsley, chopped

1 tablespoon Sherry

Salt and ground white pepper

8 boneless, skinless chicken breasts halves,

  pounded thin

Salt

1½ tablespoon black peppercorns, finely

  crushed

6 tablespoons butter or 3 tablespoons

  butter and 3 tablespoons olive oil

MORE INGREDIENTS ON NEXT PAGE

1) Dice apricots into bite cubes in a bowl, add currants and golden raisins, pour the warm stock over fruits and let it soak about 20 minutes. Drain fruit, discard liquid. Set aside.

2) In a large skillet, over medium heat, melt butter, sauté mushrooms and shallots. Cook stirring, until all water has evaporated from the mushrooms, 5 minutes.

3) Remove from skillet, add bread crumbs, and mix well. Add the fruit mixture to bread mixture, add almonds, sage, thyme, parsley, and Sherry, mix all the ingredients. Season with salt and pepper. The mixture should be slightly moist, if it feels to dry add a tablespoon of stock as needed.

4) Pound each breast between plastic wrap with a mallet. Salt and pepper each breast, add 2 tablespoons of stuffing in the center, and roll breasts around stuffing and secure with kitchen twine.

5) In a large skillet, melt butter and oil (if using) until the butter is foamy. Add the chicken breasts and cook until golden on all sides, cook 10-12 minutes more.

6) Remove the breasts from the skillet and keep warm, covered with aluminum foil.

*Continued on next page.*

*Me with my siblings, Gilles and Christine, at a Christmas party.*

*Paris, 1955*

# Paupiettes de Poulet aux Abricots Secs
## Chicken Breasts with Apricot Stuffing Continued

## CONTINUED

SAUCE:

½ cup water

⅓ cup red currant jelly

½ teaspoon orange zest

½ cup orange juice

3 tablespoons brown sugar

1 tablespoon cornstarch

3-4 tablespoons Madeira wine

Fresh sage for garnish

7) **Make the Sauce:** Combine all ingredients (except Madeira wine) in a medium saucepan, over medium-low heat. Simmer, stirring constantly, until sauce thickened and comes to a clear texture, about 5-8 minutes. Add Madeira wine and stir.

8) Remove twine from chicken and serve on a platter.

*Note:*

*This sauce recipe can be doubled. It can be made a day ahead and reheated, stirring constantly over low heat.*

# Purée de Pommes de Terre
## Mashed Potato

3 pounds Russet potatoes, peeled and
   quartered

3 tablespoons Kosher salt

¾ cup sweet butter

⅔ cup buttermilk, room temperature

¼ cup whole milk, warmed

White ground pepper

Nutmeg

1) Peel the potatoes into 1-inch chunks. Place potatoes into a large saucepan and cover with cold water, add salt.

2) Bring to a boil for 25-30 minutes or until potatoes are fork-tender.

3) Drain, and return potatoes to saucepan to dry them out.

4) Mash the potatoes with a potato masher until no lumps remain.

5) Using a spatula, gently mix in the butter, buttermilk, and whole milk until all combined.

6) Adjust seasonings with the salt and pepper.

7) Sprinkle with nutmeg and serve immediately.

# Carottes au Cognac
## Cognac-Glazed Carrots

SERVES: 8
TIME: 15 MINUTES

1½ pounds fresh carrots, peeled and sliced

6 tablespoons butter

2 tablespoons brown sugar

1 teaspoon sea salt

¼ teaspoon black pepper

2 tablespoons fresh basil, chopped
  or 2 teaspoons dried basil

½ cup Cognac

1 tablespoon maple syrup

Garnish with fresh mint

1) In a large saucepan, put carrots and add enough cold water to cover carrots. Steam carrots for 10 minutes (carrots will be firm).

2) Drain and cover with aluminum foil. Keep the carrots at room temperature.

3) In a large skillet, melt butter, with brown sugar, salt, pepper, basil, Cognac, and maple syrup.

4) Bring to a boil over high heat.

5) Reduce heat and cook, uncovered, until reduced by half, 8-10 minutes.

6) Stir in carrots, and cook on high heat tossing and turning until the carrots are glazed and heated through, 3 minutes.

7) Spoon the remaining glaze over the carrots. Garnish with chopped mint and serve immediately.

# Cerises Jubilé
## Cherries Jubilee

SERVES: 8
TIME: 25 MINUTES

**2 stick butter**

**2 cup sugar**

**2 cans (15.25 ounces) dark sweet cherries, pitted, drain and *reserve liquid***

**Zest of 2 oranges**

**Juice of 2 oranges**

**2 tablespoons corn starch**

**2 cup Brandy or Kirsch water**

**2 pint of French vanilla ice cream**

1) Drain cherries, see the note below.

2) In a large saucepan, over medium heat, melt the butter. Stir in the sugar and cook for 3 minutes or until sugar has dissolves. Add the cherries, orange juice, and orange zest.

3) Sauté for 3-4 minutes. In a small bowl, stir in cornstarch and cherry liquid together, for a sauce.

4) Pour cornstarch mixture into the cherries, and cook for 5 minutes, until it starting to thickened.

5) Remove the saucepan from the heat and pour the Brandy over the cherries. Place the pan back on the heat and carefully light up a match to flame the cherries.

6) Divide the ice cream between 8 shallow bowls.

7) Spoon the cherry sauce over the ice cream and serve immediately.

*Note:*
*You should have 2 cups of cherry liquid. If not, add cold water to make 2 cups.*

# Christmas Dinner

WINE SUGGESTION:
CABERNET SAUVIGNON OR RED BORDEAUX

# Salade d'Avocat-Pamplemousse au Saumon
## Avocado-Grapefruit Salad with Smoked Salmon

SERVES: 8

TIME: 35 MINUTES

6 large smoked salmon slices

8 white bread slices, lightly toasted

3 avocados, ripe

1 large pink grapefruit

1 lime

24 fresh tarragon leaves

3 tablespoons whipping cream

2 tablespoons Dijon mustard

5 tablespoons olive oil

1 tablespoon grapefruit juice

2 tablespoons mayonnaise

2 tablespoons black poppy seeds

Salt and pepper

1) Squeeze the limes. Chopped the tarragon, cut the avocados in half, remove their pits, with a spoon, remove the meat and cut into small dices.

2) Put the avocado meat in a bowl, and sprinkle lime juice on top, add herbs, mix delicately and set aside.

3) Peel and section the grapefruit over a bowl (reserving the juices) removing the white membranes from the sections (discard membranes). Cut the sections into third. In a bowl, mix the cream, mustard, oil, grapefruit juice, mayonnaise and salt and pepper. Set aside.

4) Cut 18 circles in the salmon slices (save leftovers). Cut 8 circles from the bread (same size as the salmon).

5) On a plate, put one bread circle, spread a thin layer of the cream mixture, top with a salmon circle, top with avocado dices, top with another salmon slice, and garnish with pieces of grapefruit and sprinkle a few poppy seeds on top of grapefruit segments.

6) Repeat the same process with the remaining bread and salmon circles. Keep refrigerated until ready to serve.

# Boeuf en Crôute
## Beef Wellington

Serves: 8
Time: 1½ hours
Oven: 425 / 400 degrees

1½ cups mushrooms, cremini, button
  or shiitake, finely chopped

¼ cup shallots, finely chopped

2 garlic cloves, minced

3 tablespoons butter

⅓ cup Madeira wine

2 tablespoons whipping cream

1 tablespoon parsley, chopped

2 sheets pastry puff, thawed in refrigerator

1- 3 pounds beef tenderloin, trimmed

Kosher salt

Ground black pepper

1 tablespoon olive oil

1 tablespoon dried thyme

4 tablespoons butter, soft

Salt and pepper

½ cup smooth liver pâté (room temperature)

½ cup fresh parsley, chopped

1 egg beaten with 1 tablespoon water
  (egg wash)

1) **Make the Druxelles Stuffing:** In a large skillet melt 2 tablespoons butter, sauté shallots until soft, add the garlic, and mushrooms and cook for 5 minutes, or until mushrooms are soft and browned.

2) Add Madeira wine, cook and stir for 5 minutes more or until wine has evaporated.

3) Stir in cream. Cook for 1 minute or until thickened, stir in parsley. Set aside.

4) **Make the Tenderloin:** Sprinkle beef with salt and pepper. Heat oil in a large Dutch oven over medium heat.

5) Add tenderloin; brown on all sides.

6) Remove from pan, and leave to cool completely.

7) Preheat oven to 425 degrees.

8) Line a baking sheet with parchment paper.

9) On a lightly floured surface, roll out the pastry dough to a large rectangle just over twice the size on the meat. Place beef on one half of dough rectangle and brush puff pastry edges with water. Spread pâté over the top of meat and sprinkle the remaining thyme and parsley.

10) Spread mushroom stuffing on top of pâté.

*Continued on next page.*

*My adorable granddaughter, Gabriella, in her kitchen.*
*She is my sous-chef in training!*
*Christmas in Los Angeles, California, 2012*

# Boeuf en Croûte
## Beef Wellington Continued

CONTINUED

11) Fold dough over to enclose meat and seal edges. Trim around three sides and, cut out a few small holes on top, to allow the steam to escape. Place on a dampened baking sheet.

12) Cut decorative shapes out of leftover dough, dip them in beaten egg and arrange on top of pastry. Glaze all over with the egg wash, chill 1 hour.

13) **Reduce oven heat to 400 degrees.**

14) Bake in hot oven for 45 to 55 minutes or until the pastry is well risen and golden or until thermometer reaches 130-135 degrees for medium rare.

15) Place on a warm serving platter, let stand for 5-10 minutes before carving into thick slices.

16) **Make the Madeira Sauce:** In a small saucepan cook ¼ cup shallots, finely chopped (2 medium) and 1 garlic clove, minced, add 2 tablespoons butter over medium heat or until shallots are soft. Stir in 2 tablespoons all-purpose flour, whisk in 1¼ cups beef broth, ¼ cup Madeira wine and ¼ cup whipping cream. Cook and stir mixture until bubbly and smooth. Stir in 1 tablespoon fresh parsley, chopped. Season to taste then pour over slices of tenderloin.

# Asperges Vertes et Blanches à l'Ail
## White and Green Asparagus in Garlic Sauce

SERVES: 8

TIME: 30 MINUTES

2 pounds green asparagus

2 pounds white asparagus

Sea salt

4 tablespoons butter

2 large shallots, chopped

Parsley, chopped

Black pepper

Garlic Sauce:

## FOR THE GARLIC SAUCE:

1 cup whipping cream

5 tablespoons mayonnaise

2 green onions, thinly sliced

4 tablespoons Dijon mustard

3 garlic cloves, minced

1) Peel the ends of the green asparagus with a potato peeler.

2) Line asparagus on a flat surface, and cut bottoms evenly. Put on a platter and cover with a wet towel until ready to use.

3) Peel the white asparagus with a potato peeler from the tip to the base. Cut bottoms evenly (same length as the green asparagus).

4) In a large pot, bring water to a boil, add sea salt, and cook white asparagus for 15-20 minutes. Drain and set aside, keep water.

5) In the same water, bring it back to a boil, add green asparagus and cook 5 minutes. Drain. Arrange asparagus in a platter and pour garlic sauce on top.

6) **Make the Garlic Sauce:** Beat whipping cream until stiffs peaks form.

7) Fold in mayonnaise, green onions, mustard and garlic. Mix well. Season with salt and pepper.

8) Spoon mixture over asparagus.

# Pommes de Terre Duchesse
## Duchess Potatoes

SERVES: 8
TIME: 45 MINUTES
OVEN: 450 DEGREES

9 medium Russet potatoes, peeled and
quartered

3 garlic cloves, halved

½ cup half and half, warmed, divided

8 tablespoons sweet butter, room
   temperature

2 large egg yolks, room temperature

2 teaspoons kosher salt

¼ teaspoon white pepper

½ cup Swiss cheese, grated

Freshly grated nutmeg

1) Preheat oven to 450 degrees.

2) In a large saucepan, add potato chunks and just enough cold water to cover potatoes.

3) Bring to a boil. Reduce heat to medium; cover and let simmer for 20-25 minutes or until potatoes are tender when pierced with a knife.

4) Remove from heat and drain potatoes thoroughly in a colander. Return potatoes to pan; heat over medium-low heat for 1-2 minutes to dry potatoes, stirring occasionally.

5) Mash potatoes with a food mill or a potato masher until they are smooth and free of any lumps. Add ¼ cup half-and-half, butter, egg yolks, salt and pepper, and nutmeg, mix well to blend. Slowly add cheese and remaining half and half to the potatoes (you may not need all of the cream, you don't want the potatoes to be too soft or wet, or they won't hold their shape). The potatoes should be stiff.

6) Place a large star tip in a pastry bag and fill bag with mixture. Pipe potatoes into 8 mounds on a parchment-lined baking sheet. Sprinkle each mound with additional nutmeg.

7) Bake in hot oven for 10-12 minutes or until lightly browned.

8) Serve immediately.

# Charlotte au Chocolat
## Chocolate Charlotte Mousse

SERVES: 8 - 10

TIME: 30 MINUTES + 8 HOURS CHILL TIME

2-8 ounces milk chocolate bars, like

   Hershey's

2 blocks (2 ounces) unsweetened baking

   chocolate, like Hershey's

5 tablespoons water

2 tablespoons Brandy

2 large egg yolks

¼ cup sweet butter

1 cup heavy cream

18-24 ladyfingers, split in half

Zest of ½ an orange

4 large egg whites

4 tablespoons raspberry jam

Chopped almonds

Chopped pistachios

## FOR THE RASPBERRY *PURÉE*:

2 cups of fresh raspberries

¼ cup water

½ cup sugar

3 tablespoons of blackberry liquor,

   like Chambord

1) Break chocolate bars and baking chocolate into small pieces. Melt chocolate with water and Rum in top double boiler over hot, not boiling water; stir until smooth.

2) Remove from the heat; blend in egg yolks. Add butter, 1 tablespoon at a time, stirring until blended, add orange zest. Cool slightly.

3) Whip cream until stiff, carefully fold into chocolate mixture. Chill 1 hour or until mousse begins to set.

4) Spread each bottom of the ladyfingers with the raspberry jam. Line the bottom of 8 to 9 inch spring form pan with the jammed ladyfingers. Line the side with the rounded side against the pan.

5) Beat egg whites until stiff but not dry. Fold into the chocolate mixture. Pour into ladyfinger-lined pan. Refrigerate until set at least 5-8 hours or overnight.

6) Just before serving, remove side of pan, transfer the dessert to a platter.

7) Spread 3 tablespoons of *purée* on each plate, place a slice of charlotte on top, add whipped cream, and decorate with fresh cranberries (or raspberries) and pistachios.

8) **Make the *Purée*:** Pour raspberries, water, and sugar into a medium saucepan. Let simmer for 20 minutes, stirring occasionally, until all berries are soft. Remove from heat and let the mixture cool down. Strain berries in a sieve and push through with a wooden spoon. Add blackberry liquor and mix well. Keep refrigerated until ready to use.

# Dinner for Two by the Fire

WINE SUGGESTION:
CHAMPAGNE OR CHABLIS

# Huîtres à la Sauce Mignonette
## Oysters in Shallot Sauce

SERVES: 2
TIME: 30 MINUTES

10 blue oysters, cold

1 cup red wine vinegar

1 tablespoon black peppercorns, crushed

4 shallots, finely minced

1)  Open oysters, and remove any shells or sand with a brush.

2)  Combine vinegar, peppercorns and shallots in a jar.

3)  Serve oysters on a bed of sea salt, spoon 1 tablespoon of shallot sauce in each.

4)  Garnish with lemon wedges and serve immediately.

*Note:*
*Keep refrigerated for up to a month.*

# Velouté de Champignons
## Creamy Mushroom Soup

SERVES: 2

TIME: 45 MINUTES

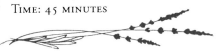

2 tablespoons butter

½ sweet onion, finely chopped

1 leek, white part only, cleaned and
    finely chopped

½ pound fresh button mushrooms,
    finely chopped

¼ cup shiitake mushrooms, finely chopped

Salt and white pepper

1 tablespoon cornstarch

3 cups chicken broth

1 cup whipping cream

1 tablespoon Sherry

Fresh parsley

2 mushroom slices

1) In a medium saucepan, melt butter, sauté onion and leek until soft.

2) Add the mushrooms, salt and pepper, pour the chicken broth in saucepan and bring to a simmer for 20 minutes.

3) Put soup in blender and *purée* until smooth.

4) Pour soup back in saucepan, add Sherry, dilute the cornstarch with the cream add to soup, mix well.

5) Increase heat to medium-low, stirring constantly, until soup thickens, 8 minutes.

6) Garnish with parsley and a mushroom slice.

*Note:*
*Cheese Straws go great with this recipe.*
*To find my recipe for Cheese Straws, go to: cafedion.com*

# Salade César au Homard
## Caesar Salad with Lobster

SERVES: 2
TIME: 25 MINUTES

3 lobster tails, cooked

Lemon juice

Salt and pepper

### FOR THE CÉSAR:

2 anchovies

1 small garlic clove, minced

Pinch of sea salt

1 egg yolk, room temperature

1 tablespoon fresh lemon juice

½ teaspoon Dijon mustard

1 tablespoon olive oil

¼ cup vegetable oil

2 tablespoons Parmesan cheese, grated

Ground black pepper

1 large romaine salad, chopped into
    large chunks

2 tablespoons Swiss cheese or shaving
    of fresh Parmesan cheese

1) Chop together: anchovies, garlic and salt, using the side of knife blade, mash all ingredients into a thin paste, scrape into a large salad bowl, whisk egg yolk, lemon juice and mustard, adding drops of olive oil, then adding vegetable oil slowly, whisk until dressing is thick and glossy, whisk in Parmesan cheese.

2) Season with salt and pepper. Add more lemon juice if needed.

3) Break romaine with your fingers.

4) Toss lettuce with croutons and dressing.

5) **Make the Croutons:** Tearing fresh bread will ensure the dressing to go into the crannies of the pieces. Toss 1 cup of torn bread into 1-inch thick, with 2 tablespoons olive oil, on a rimmed baking sheet, season with sea salt and ground black pepper, mix well. Bake in oven at 375 degrees, tossing occasionally until golden, 15-20 minutes.

6) **Prepare the Lobster:** Remove the lobster meat, pulling it off the shell and reserve meat. Disregard tube-like limbs. Discard body and shells. Cut the tails in medallions, squeeze lemon juice, and sprinkle with salt and pepper, set aside.

7) To serve, spread salad on each dinner plate, place one and half of the medallions on top of salad.

8) Garnish with Parmesan shavings and lemon wedges.

# Poires Pôchées avec Sauce Grand-Marnier
## Poached Pear with Grand-Marnier Sauce

SERVES: 2

TIME: 45 MINUTES

2 ripe medium pears, peeled and cored

2 cups water

¾ cup sugar

1 teaspoon vanilla extract

1 egg yolk, beaten

1 tablespoon orange liqueur, like

  Grand-Marnier

½ cup whipping cream

For garnish: fresh mint, 4 fresh cranberries

or raspberries, dark chocolate sauce

1) Peel the pears. Leave the stems on, then core pears from the bottom (wide ends).

2) To poach pears, in a medium saucepan bring the 2 cups of water and ½ cup sugar to a boil. Carefully add the pears, stems up. Reduce heat. Cover and simmer for 20 minutes or until pears are tender. Remove from heat and let the pears cool in liquid.

3) In top of a double boiler combine egg yolk, 1 tablespoon water, and the remaining ¼ cup sugar. Place the top of the double boiler over, but not touching the water, gently boiling water.

4) Beat with electric mixer on medium speed for 5 minutes or until the mixture is very fluffy, thick and a pale yellow. Immediately stir Grand-Marnier. Let cool for 12 minutes.

5) Wash the beaters, in another bowl beat whipping cream till stiff peaks form. Fold whipped cream into egg mixture.

6) Remove the pears from liquid and drain well. Spoon some sauce onto dessert plates. Place pears on top of sauce, then spoon remaining sauce on top of pears.

7) Garnish with mint, cranberries or raspberries and chocolate sauce.

*Note:*
*Find a great recipe for Chocolate Sauce on my*
*website, cafedion.com*

# Elegant Christmas Buffet

WINE SUGGESTION:
EGGNOG, WHITE CHARDONNAY

# Soupe de Courge
## Butternut Squash Soup

SERVES: 8
TIME: 50 MINUTES

1 medium sweet onion, chopped

3 celery ribs, chopped

2 large carrots, peeled and chopped

1 bay leaf

2½ pounds butternut squash, peeled and chopped

3 medium potatoes, peeled and chopped

3½ cups chicken stock

⅔ cup heavy cream

⅔ cup milk

4 tablespoons maple syrup

3 tablespoons Sherry or Brandy

Sea salt and white pepper

Fresh basil, chopped, for garnish

1) In a large Dutch oven, melt butter over medium heat, sauté onion, celery, and carrots, stir.

2) Add bay leaf, squash and potatoes. Cook for 20 minutes, add chicken stock and bring to a boil.

3) Reduce heat, cover and simmer for 20-30 minutes or until vegetables are soft.

4) Remove from heat, cool slightly and use an immersion blender or regular blender, to *purée* the vegetables.

5) Return the soup to the stove and reheat the soup in the Dutch oven over low heat.

6) Add cream, milk, maple syrup, and Sherry. Season with salt and pepper. Simmer for 5 minutes.

7) Garnish with a basil.

# Dinde Rôtie au Jus
## Roasted Turkey with Gravy

SERVES: 8
TIME: 4 HOURS
OVEN: 425 DEGREES

1 fresh turkey, 14-16 pounds

¼ cup vegetable oil

Salt and pepper

½ stick butter, soft

1 lemon

1 small onion, whole

2 garlic cloves, crushed

2 bay leaves

Fresh rosemary and fresh thyme

## FOR THE GRAVY:

Turkey neck and giblets

8 cups chicken broth, low sodium

1 large onion, quartered

2 celery ribs with leaves

1 lemon, quartered

¼ cup all-purpose flour

Salt and pepper

1) Preheat oven to 425 degrees.

2) Wipe turkey with a damp cloth and rub the body with oil. Massage butter all over turkey

3) Sprinkle with salt and pepper. Fill the cavity with lemon, onion, garlic cloves, bay leaves, rosemary and thyme. Tie the cavity with kitchen twine.

4) Place the turkey breasts down on a rack in a roasting pan. Let it rest for 10 minutes.

5) For the stock: in a large saucepan, put the neck, gizzards and heart (do not use the liver), cover with chicken stock, onion, celery, thyme, garlic. Bring to boil then reduce to a simmer for 2 hours, skimming the fat from the surface; add more stock if needed.

6) Drain the stock, discard solids.

7) Roast the turkey for 40 minutes, basting with chicken stock every 20 minutes. Lower oven heat to 325 degrees. Tent the turkey with foil, keep basting every 20 minutes. Roast the turkey for 1 hour.

8) Turn the turkey over, breast side up and roast another hour. Keep on basting.

9) Place the stuffing in the oven, covered, 1 hour before the turkey is done.

*Continued on next page.*

*A Christmas party with friends at my parents' house.*
*Bellevue, 1969*

# Dinde Rôtie au Jus
## Roasted Turkey with Gravy Continued

## CONTINUED

10) Remove the turkey for the roasting pan, cover with foil and let it rest for 20 minutes. Drain the juices for the roasting pan, keeping the brown pits and discarding the fat.

11) In the roasting pan, add the flour and whish adding a ladle of the warm chicken stock at a time, use remaining chicken stock. Season with salt and pepper to taste. Pour into a gravy boat and garnish fresh parsley.

*Note:*
*The recommended cooking time for turkey is 20 minutes per pound.*
*Remember to remove the neck and giblets before cooking the turkey. Also remove package from the neck cavity.*

# Farce
## Stuffing

SERVES: 8

TIME: 55 MINUTES

OVEN: 350 DEGREES

6 tablespoons butter, divided

1 large sweet onion, chopped

2 garlic cloves, minced

1½ cups mushrooms, chopped

1 cup celery, chopped

1 Jimmy Dean pork sausage with sage,
   crumbed

1 tablespoon poultry seasonings

⅛ teaspoon dried thyme

⅛ teaspoon dried rosemary

2 large eggs

Salt and ground black pepper to taste

1 cup regular bread crumbs

½ cup chicken stock or more

¼ cup golden raisins

¼ cup dried cranberries

1 green apple, diced

¼ cup walnuts, chopped

2 tablespoons fresh sage, chopped

1)  In a large skillet, melt 2 tablespoons butter, sauté onion and garlic until translucent, add mushrooms and cook until all the water has evaporated.

2)  Remove for skillet to a large bowl. Set aside. In same skillet melt 2 tablespoons butter and sauté celery, until soft. Add celery to mushroom mixture.

3)  Sauté remaining butter and cook sausage until all pink is gone (golden brown). Season with herbs. Transfer sausage to mushroom mixture. Mix all ingredients well. Add eggs, salt and pepper, bread crumbs, add chicken stock until all ingredients are moist (not wet).

4)  Add raisins, cranberries, green apple, fresh sage and walnuts, mix well.

5)  Transfer mixture to a buttered baking dish, cover with aluminum foil and bake in the oven for 30 minutes. Remove foil and continue baking for another 10 minutes.

6)  Serve immediately.

*Note:*
*You can cook this stuffing with the turkey, 1 hour before the turkey is done.*

# Conserve d'Airelles Rouges
## Red Cranberry Preserve

SERVES: 8

TIME: 45 MINUTES

2 large thin-skinned seedless oranges

1 cup water

½ cup sugar

3 cups fresh cranberries (12 ounces)

¼ cup walnuts, chopped

2 tablespoons Cointreau or Triple Sec

2 tablespoons fresh parsley, chopped

1 tablespoon fresh mint, chopped

1) Grate 1 tablespoon of orange zest, set aside.

2) Peel and section oranges over a bowl, reserving juices and membranes.

3) Squeeze membranes to extract all the juices. Discard membranes and set oranges aside.

4) Combine water, sugar in a medium saucepan. Bring water to a boil, add cranberries and cook for 5 minutes, over medium heat, stirring occasionally.

5) Add orange sections, and orange juice cook for 15 minutes or until thickened, stirring frequently.

6) Remove from heat, add orange zest, walnuts, Cointreau and parsley, mix well.

7) Spoon into a bowl, cover with plastic wrap and chill until ready to serve.

8) Garnish with mint.

# Purée de Patates Douces au Sirop d'Èrable
## Mashed Sweet Potato with Maple Syrup

4 pounds medium sweet potatoes, peeled
and cut into 1-inch chunks

Kosher salt

1 cup low-fat Greek yogurt or heavy cream

2 teaspoons orange zest

2 tablespoons orange juice

1 teaspoon salt

Ground white pepper

½ cup buttermilk

2 tablespoons maple syrup

3 tablespoons butter

¼ teaspoon nutmeg, grated

1) Put the potatoes in a large pot, cover with cold water by 1 inch. Add a pinch of kosher salt.

2) Bring to a simmer over medium-high heat. Simmer until very tender, 15-18 minutes. Test with a knife, it should go through very easily.

3) Drain and return to pot over low heat to help dry the potatoes, add the yogurt, orange zest, orange juice, salt, pepper and buttermilk, mash well, using a potato masher (do not use blender), until smooth and creamy.

4) Add maple syrup, and butter, mix well.

5) Sprinkle with nutmeg and adjust other seasonings if needed.

# Petits Pois, Carottes, Champignons Grillés
## Grilled Peas, Carrots, Mushrooms

SERVES: 8

TIME: 35 MINUTES

1 large carrot, sliced

1-10 ounces package baby French peas

2 tablespoons butter

1 garlic clove, minced

3 cups fresh mushrooms, sliced

2 green onions, chopped

2 tablespoons fresh basil, chopped

¼ teaspoon sea salt

Ground black pepper to taste

1) In a medium saucepan cook carrots, covered in a small amount of boiling salted water, for 3 minutes.

2) Add frozen peas. Return to boiling; reduce heat.

3) Cook for 5 minutes longer or until carrots are tender. Drain well. Remove carrots and peas from pan. Set aside.

4) In the same pan, melt butter and sauté mushrooms, garlic and green onions until tender. Stir in basil, salt, and pepper. Return carrots and peas to pan; heat through, stirring occasionally.

5) Serve immediately.

# Petits Gâteaux aux Fruits Secs
## Mini Fruit Cakes

SERVES: 24
TIME: 40 MINUTES
OVEN: 400 DEGREES

2 cups raisins

¼ cup rum (dark)

1½ cups fruit cake mix

½ cup rum (dark)

1½ sticks butter, room temperature

1 cup sugar

3 large eggs, room temperature

2 cups all-purpose flour

1 teaspoon baking soda

Zest of 1 orange and juice of ½ orange

1 tablespoon vanilla or almond extract

1) Preheat oven to 400 degrees.

2) Soak raisins in hot water for 5 minutes. Drain. Soak raisins in rum.

3) Soak mix fruits in ¼ cup rum; let stand for 25 minutes.

4) In a large bowl of a food processor, mix together butter and sugar to a pale yellow, add the eggs, one by one, pour the flour in small amount at a time, add baking powder, whisking all ingredients.

5) Mix raisins and dried fruit mixture together.

6) To the butter mixture, add fruit mixture, orange zest, orange juice, vanilla extract, and mix well.

7) Pour the dough into paper cup lined muffin tins. Bake in the hot oven for 5 minutes.

8) **Lower the oven heat to 375 degrees** and bake for 10-20 minutes longer.

*Note:*
*Do not open oven door for the first 15 minutes; otherwise, the dough could fall.*

# *Bûche de Noël*
## *Christmas Log*

SERVES: 8
TIME: 2 HOURS
OVEN: 425 DEGREES

## SPONGE CAKE:

4 egg whites, room temperature

½ cup sugar

8 eggs, room temperature, separated

¼ teaspoon salt

Zest of a lemon

⅔ cup cake flour

3 tablespoons cornstarch

## BUTTERCREAM FILLING:

½ cup water

1 cup superfine sugar

1 vanilla bean or 1 teaspoon vanilla extract

6 egg yolks, room temperature

⅓ cup unsweetened cocoa, sifted

3 ounces semisweet chocolate, melted
   and warmed

2 tablespoons powdered instant coffee
   (diluted in 2 tablespoons warm water)

3 sticks sweet butter, room temperature

## MERINGUE MUSHROOMS:

1 egg white

¼ cup superfine sugar

¼ teaspoon vanilla extract

1 ounce semisweet chocolate melted

2 tablespoons cocoa

1)  Preheat oven to 425 degrees.

2)  **Make Sponge Cake:** Beat egg whites until stiff peaks formed, add sugar one tablespoon at a time, whisking until all the sugar is incorporated.

3)  In a bowl, whisk the egg yolks, salt, lemon zest together until well blended. Gradually fold egg yolk mixture into egg white mixture, fold gently. Sift flour and cornstarch and fold lightly into egg mixture.

4)  Line a jelly-roll pan with parchment paper. Spread mixture evenly over the bottom of pan with a long spatula or a cake scraper.

5)  Bake for 5-8 minutes or until center of the cake springs back when lightly pressing top of cake. Note: Check cake after 5 minutes of cooking (each oven is different.)

6)  Sprinkle towel with powder sugar. Run tip of knife around inside edge of pan to release cake. Invert cake onto towel, peel off the paper and roll cake in towel, jelly-roll type style.

7)  Alternatively, once cooled down, leave cake flat and cover with a damp towel.

8)  Spread flavored butter cream over cake to within ¼ inch of edges. Re-roll without the towel, and dust with powder sugar or spread icing over log. Decorate as you wish.

*Continued on next page.*

*My granddaughter, Madison, learning to make a ginger bread house*

*and the Bûche de Noël. Looks great! Boulder, Colorado, 2011*

# Bûche de Noël
## Christmas Log Continued

9) Keep in the refrigerator until ready to serve. Let it stand at room temperature for ½ hour before cutting.

10) **Make the Butter Cream:** Place sugar, vanilla, ⅓ cup cold water in medium saucepan over moderate heat and bring to a boil; boil syrup until temperature reaches 240 degrees F. (soft ball stage) on a candy thermometer.

11) Beat egg yolks in a mixing bowl until frothy.

12) Remove vanilla bean (if using) from syrup and pour in slow, steady stream into egg yolks, beating constantly on high with electric mixer. Continue beating until mixture has cooled down.

13) Cream butter until very light and fluffy, add egg yolk mixture to butter gradually, beating constantly. Beat until mixture is thick and fluffy. Add cocoa, chocolate, and coffee in butter, mix well.

14) Spread half of the butter cream over cake, roll cake back and place on silver platter, seam side down. Spread a thin layer of butter cream over the rolled cake.

15) **Make the Meringue Mushrooms:** Preheat oven to 275 degrees.

16) Grease 1 baking sheet, line with parchment paper

*Continued on next page.*

*From top to bottom:*

*1. My daughter, Francine, on her first Christmas. Bowie, Maryland, 1966*

*2. Francine's second Christmas with my mother and sister, Françoise. Bowie, Maryland, 1967*

# Bûche de Noël
## Christmas Log Continued

**CONTINUED**

17) In a clean, grease-free bowl, beat egg white until very stiff, but not dry. Add ½ teaspoon of sugar, beat until incorporated and meringue is stiff and shiny. Add remaining sugar, a little at a time, beating well after each addition. Beat in vanilla. Spoon mixture in a large piping bag fitted with a ½-inch plain tip.

18) To make mushrooms caps: pipe 10-15 rounded mounds, about 1-inch in diameter on baking sheet.

19) To make the stalks: pipe 10-15 pyramids-shaped blocks.

20) Bake for 1 hour or until dry. Let them cool on the baking sheet. Remove each cap, cut a small hole in the flat side, fill hole with dab of chocolate. Invert pointed ends of stalks into chocolate holes.

21) Leave mushrooms upright and sprinkle with cocoa. Use the mushrooms to decorate the log.

# Romantic New Year's Eve Supper

WINE SUGGESTION: CHILLED ROSE WINE

# Escargots à l'Ail et au Persil Beurré
## Snails in Garlic and Parsley Butter

SERVES: 2
TIME: 40 MINUTES
OVEN: 450 DEGREES

## ESCARGOTS:

3 tablespoons butter

4 ounces shallots, finely minced

12 Burgundy snails, rinsed under running

cold water, dried on paper towels

2 large garlic cloves, peeled and

  finely chopped

2 tablespoons Cognac, warmed

Salt and pepper

## GARLIC AND PARSLEY BUTTER:

1 stick of butter, room temperature

1 teaspoon fine sea salt

1 teaspoon ground black pepper

2 large garlic cloves

3 tablespoons fresh parsley, chopped

*1)* **Make the *Escargots*:** Melt the butter in a medium saucepan over low heat and sauté shallots, snails and garlic, for 12 minutes. Pour in Cognac and simmer for 2 minutes longer. Season with salt and pepper, and mix well. Set aside and let cool.

*2)* **Make the Garlic and Parsley Butter:** Mix together butter, sea salt, pepper, parsley and garlic in a medium bowl, work the butter with a wooden spoon until the butter become a paste. Adjust seasonings if needed.

*3)* In a 6-snail gratin dish, divide half of the garlic butter among the dishes. Place one snail in each hole of the dish, and then cover with the remaining garlic butter.

*4)* Bake until butter is melted and sizzling, about 4-6 minutes.

*5)* Serve immediately with crusty French baguette.

# Vol-au-Vent de Fruits de Mer
## Seafood in Puff Pastry

SERVES: 2
TIME: 1 HOUR
OVEN: 420 DEGREES

1 sheet frozen puff pastry, thawed in
   refrigerator overnight

Flour for dusting

4 large shrimp, cleaned, deveined and cut
   into quarters

½ cup seafood shreds (imitation crab)
   shredded

¼ cup bay scallop

1 lobster tail, diced

¼ cup butter

2 tablespoons shallots, chopped

4 tablespoons mushrooms, finely chopped

3 tablespoons flour

¾ cup heavy cream

1 tablespoon Sherry

¼ cup asparagus, tips only and steamed

¼ cup frozen peas, thaw

Salt and pepper

1½ tablespoon dill

2 tablespoons fresh parsley, chopped

1) Preheat oven to 420 degrees.

2) On a floured surface, roll puff pastry to ½ inch thick. Cut 2 round circles (4 inches).

3) Using a small circle (2.5 inches), place the circle on the center of the larger circle to create a top. Pour the circles onto a moist and cold baking sheet.

4) Bake in hot oven for 10-20 minutes. The puff pastry shells should be puffy and golden. Turn off the oven, but keep them in the oven so they stay warm (keep oven door slightly open).

5) In a medium saucepan, put 1 cup water, ½ small onion, 1 celery stalk, 1 bay leaf, 2 slices of lemon, ¼ cup white wine, bring to slow boil, add shrimp, crab, scallops, and lobster tail pieces, gently simmer, covered for 5 minutes. Drain and **reserve liquid**.

6) In a large saucepan, melt the butter, sauté shallots, mushrooms, until tender, stirring often.

7) Remove from heat, stir in flour and pepper, and blend well. Gradually stir in cream, bring to boil, stirring often, reduce heat to a simmer, add Sherry, ½ of shrimp liquid, asparagus, and peas, cook on low heat for 5 minutes, if sauce appears to thick, add more shrimp liquid, add the shrimp mixture, mix well. Simmer for a couple minutes.

8) Add dill and parsley, stir.

9) With the tip of a knife, remove the top of each pastry. Fill the shells with the shrimp mixture. Place the top back on, and serve immediately.

# Petits Haricots Verts aux Noix

## Green Beans with Pecans

SERVES: 2

TIME: 20 MINUTES

1 package (9 ounces) frozen French style
green beans

1 tablespoon butter, room temperature

1 shallot, chopped

¼ cup pecans, chopped

Fresh parsley, chopped

Juice of ½ a lemon

1)  Cook green beans according to package directions.

2)  Drain.

3)  In a large skillet, melt the butter and cook shallots until soft.

4)  Toss beans in butter, add pecans.

5)  Garnish with parsley and squeeze lemon juice on top of beans.

# Mousse au Chocolat
## Chocolate Mousse

SERVES: 2

TIME: 20 MINUTES + COOL TIME

1¼ ounces bittersweet chocolate,
 finely chopped

½ tablespoon sweet butter

½ tablespoon espresso coffee, cold

½ teaspoon vanilla extract

¼ cup heavy cream

1 egg, separated

¼ tablespoon sugar

1 teaspoon Kahlua liquor

Fresh strawberries, whipped cream
 and fresh mint for garnish

1) Combine chocolate, butter and coffee in a double boiler over medium heat. Stir until smooth. Remove from heat and let it cool until still warm to the touch.

2) Mix egg yolk into warm chocolate mixture, and add Kahlua liquor.

3) In a separate bowl, whip the heavy cream until soft peaks formed, add vanilla extract, whipping a few seconds more. Keep cold until ready to use.

4) In a smaller bowl, whip egg white until foamy, add sugar. Continue whipping until soft peaks form.

5) Gently fold ⅓ of the whipped cream into chocolate mixture. Add half of the egg white, incorporate them, add the second half.

6) Finally add the remaining whipped cream and fold until there are no more white streaks.

7) Spoon into serving glass bowls, cover and refrigerate for at least 5 hours.

8) Garnish with strawberries, whipped cream and mint.

# Tuiles
## Almond Cookies

SERVES: 12 - 18
TIME: 1½ HOURS
OVEN: 365 DEGREES

½ cup all-purpose flour

½ cup powdered sugar

⅛ teaspoon salt

3 egg whites

4 tablespoons sweet butter, melted

¼ teaspoon almond extract

½ cup sliced almonds, roasted

1) Preheat oven to 365 degrees.

2) Line a large baking sheet with parchment paper and set aside.

3) In a mixing bowl, whisk flour, sugar, and salt.

4) Whisk in the egg whites, butter and almond extract until well blended.

5) Let the batter seat for 45 minutes at room temperature.

6) Drop rounded tablespoons of batter about 6 inches apart onto the lined baking sheet.

7) Spread the batter with the back of a spoon into 5-inch circles.

8) Sprinkle each circle with sliced almonds and bake in middle of oven until golden between 8- 10 minutes.

9) With a thin spatula, quickly remove the cookies 1 at a time and drape them on a rolling pan or bottle to create the shape of a *tuile* (if the cookie becomes to brittle, re-place on baking sheet and place in oven for 15 seconds to soften).

10) Cool the *tuiles* on the rolling pan, gently lift off and transfer to a platter until ready to use.

From left to right:

1. Me with my mother and my daughter. Clichy, Paris, 1978

2. Our granddaughter, Madison, making Christmas breakfast.
   Boulder, Colorado, 2009

# *Recipe Index*

*Christmas happiness!*
*My granddaughter, Madison, on Christmas Day.*
*Boulder, Colorado, 2011*

| | |
|---|---|
| **Apricot glaze:** | reduced, strained apricot jam to coat cakes or pastries |
| **Au gratin:** | to form a crust made of bread or grated cheese |
| **Bain-marie:** | a double boiler; two pots are nestled together so that the top is gently heated by the simmering water in the bottom pot |
| **Beurre manié:** | in a bowl, mix 3 tablespoons all-purpose flour and 3 tablespoons soft butter into a paste. Gently whisk into any sauce to thicken. Makes a great thickener. |
| **Boeuf:** | beef |
| **Boissons:** | drinks |
| **Bouquet garni:** | fresh herbs tied together with kitchen twine. Usually parsley, thyme, rosemary and bay leaf |
| **Chevre:** | goat |
| **Court-bouillon:** | clear, strong stock or broth |
| **Caramel:** | sugar melted to a medium-brown color |
| **Crème Chantilly:** | in a bowl, combine 1½ cups chilled whipping cream, ¾ cup confectioner's sugar and 1 teaspoon vanilla extract. Whisk with hand mixer until soft peaks form. Sweeten whipped cream with any liqueur. |
| **Côquille:** | scallop shell which is often used as a plate for presentation of seafood dishes |
| **Coulis:** | a thick sauce, such as a *purée* of fresh fruit |
| **Crôuton:** | small cubes of bread fried in butter. Often served in soups or salads or used as a garnish |
| **Dinde:** | turkey |
| **Egg Wash:** | mix together 1 egg and 1 tablespoon water |
| **Entrée:** | main dish |
| **Ficelle:** | kitchen twine |
| **Haricots verts:** | green beans |
| **Julienne:** | cut in fine, short strips |
| **Lardon:** | a strip of pork or bacon sautéed in a hot skillet and used for salads or meat dishes |
| **Médallion:** | round slice of meat |
| **Mince:** | cut in small pieces |
| **Mûre:** | blackberry |
| **Pearl onion:** | to peel a pearl onion, trim the root ends of the onions. Blanch them in boiling water for 1-2 minutes, and transfer them to an ice water bowl. Pinch each onion, and they will slip out of their skins. |
| **Plat d'accompagnement:** | side dish |
| **Poulet:** | chicken |
| **Purée:** | a smooth, creamy substance made of liquidized or crushed vegetables or fruit. |
| **Reduce:** | to boil down a sauce or liquid until it thickens to the consistency desired |
| **Sauté:** | to cook small amounts of meats or vegetables in very hot fat |
| **Simmer:** | to cook at very low heat |
| **Veau:** | veal |
| **Vinaigrette:** | a salad dressing made with oil, vinegar and mustard |
| **Zest:** | the grated peel of citrus fruit |

# Biography

Dion Jones-Lewin was born in Paris France. Her grandmother, Germaine Dethiere, was a classically-trained French chef who developed the technique of *Français simple* or "simple French." After Germaine accepted a chef's position in England, Dion would spend her summer vacations there, where under Germaine's tutelage, Dion studied the art of classic French cooking. When Germaine returned to Paris, Dion continued studying classic French cooking and completed her formal training in all aspects of French cooking.

In the 1970's, Dion moved to Hawaii where she experimented with island cuisine. She remained in Hawaii for eleven years before moving to Boulder, Colorado, where she opened a French cooking school, *Ecole de Cuisine*. Over a two-year period, she trained several hundred students in *La Methode*, the art of French cooking, as developed by her *grand-mère*.

Dion still resides in Boulder, but because she is a *Parisienne* at heart, she returns to *Le Cordon Bleu* in Paris twice a year for continued training. She is working on a series of cookbooks derived from her grandmother's original recipes, of which this is the second.

Dion also has her own website, www.CafeDion.com, dedicated to classic French cooking made simple. It is an informative blog, which is updated weekly, and designed to accompany her cookbook series.

# Acknowledgements

This book could not be what it is without the help of my friends and colleagues. *Merci beaucoup* to Jenny Orin for her beautiful photography, design and support; My "bookies" friends for their enthusiasium. Colette Roynel for her constant words of encouragement every time she calls me from Paris. To my husband Derek for his encouragement and support; and finally to my *grand-mère*, Germaine Jones. If it were not for her devotion to me and her culinary skills, this book series would not exist.

I love you all very much,
*Merci de tout coeur.*

*Dion Jones-Lewin*
BOULDER, COLORADO

*From top to bottom:*

*1. My mother and my cousins, René and Liliane. Clichy, Paris, 1961*

*2. My mother and family; Cousin Simone, Francoise, Gilles, Tata Julie, and Tonton Jean. Clichy, Paris, 1961*

# Testimonials

"I love marinades and can't wait to get my vegetables and chicken married to your recipes for the summer grill. My taste buds are so eager. Love your blog, and I just purchased Vol. II. Ooo lah lah! I went right home and was able to prepare something for lunch quickly and easily. So yum. I want to own all your recipe books. The convenient size is handy for taking grocery shopping. Much love and much success. "
- *Holly from Boulder, Colorado*

"Last night I had a look into the Sealed Box! I decided to have today the tuna salad with a German variety of mesclum salad. Next time we have something to celebrate we will have the Pear Belle Helene!"
- *Edda from Germany*

"My granddaughter and friend (and my daughter) came over to swim. When they came in, they smelled your pea soup, and had to have some before we went to the pool!!! They loved it!!!! We are all enjoying your recipes."
- *Jean Bradley from Longmont, CO*

"Dion, what a great cookbook! Beautiful layout and pictures. Just made your cheese biscuits. Delicious and *tres simple!* Looking forward to the next in the series."
- *Daniel J from California*

"This book is absolutely wonderful. The recipes are delicious and are easy to follow. I gave this book as a gift to a friend of mine who is a culinary fanatic and she thought the recipes were fantastic. I had never tackled French cuisine in the past because it always appeared daunting to me. However, this book makes it so easy and effortless. In my friends' words, "each dish looks so simple with its simple list of ingredients." My friend's husband, who loves to bake, said "the Rum Cake with Raisins and Whipped Cream was by far the best I have ever come across. "
- *Sarom from Connecticut*

*"Sieht wirklich lecker! Vielen Dank fur Ihre Rezept, werde diesen ein sehr, sehr bald ausprobieren!"*
"Looks really delicious! Thank you for your recipe, will try this one very, very soon!"
- *Tina Williams from Germany*

"Dion, Thank you for sharing the delicious easy to follow recipes that even this German-Irish gal can create! The gorgeous cover on your new book will make it the first cookbook to jump out of every baker's collection. You are such an inspiration! Much success with "From the Sealed Box", I will spread the butter, er, I mean spread the word. :)"
- *Judy Murphy from Las Vegas, Nevada*

"The recipes in both volumes of 'From the Sealed Box' are wonderful and easy to follow. I cannot wait for volume 3! My friends actually think I'm a good cook - I've never received so many compliments and I've been cooking for a very long time."
- *Joy from Longmont, Colorado*

# Measurements & Conversions

| | | |
|---|---|---|
| 1 teaspoon | = | ⅓ tablespoon |
| 1 tablespoon | = | 3 teaspoons |
| 2 tablespoons | = | ⅛ cup (1 ounce) |
| 4 tablespoons | = | ¼ cup |
| 5⅓ tablespoons | = | ⅓ cup |
| 8 tablespoons | = | ½ cup |
| 16 tablespoons | = | 1 cup |
| ⅜ cup | = | 5 tablespoons |
| 1 cup | = | ½ pint |
| 2 cups | = | 1 pint |
| 2 pints | = | 1 quart |
| 4 quarts | = | 1 gallon |
| 1 pound | = | 16 ounces |
| 1 fluid ounce | = | 2 tablespoons |
| 16 fluid ounces | = | 1 pint |
| 1 pint | = | 2 cups |
| 2 pints | = | 4 cups (1 quart) |
| 4 quarts | = | 16 cups (1 gallon) |